Poetry and Illustrations by Koko Escoto

I'M

STILL

HEALING

A poetry collection of love and trauma.

Koko Escoto

ISBN: 979-8-9883051-2-5 (Paperback)
ISBN: 979-8-9883051-0-1 (Ebook)
ISBN: 979-8-9883051-1-8 (Audiobook)

Book Cover by Koko Escoto.
Illustrations by Koko Escoto.

Subscribe to Koko Escoto's newsletter:

DEDICATION

To the lovers and the helpers.
Those who have been in relationships
that swallowed them whole.
You deserved better.

ACKNOWLEDGEMENTS

Thank you to the community I found on TikTok.

My sweet oranges,
I wouldn't have thought this book was possible
without your love and support.

I also want to extend a thank you to my sister and
brother-in-law, Amy and Rudy Aguilar, for the advice and
encouragement.

TABLE OF CONTENTS

I'm Still Healing - Koko Escoto

THE LOVE

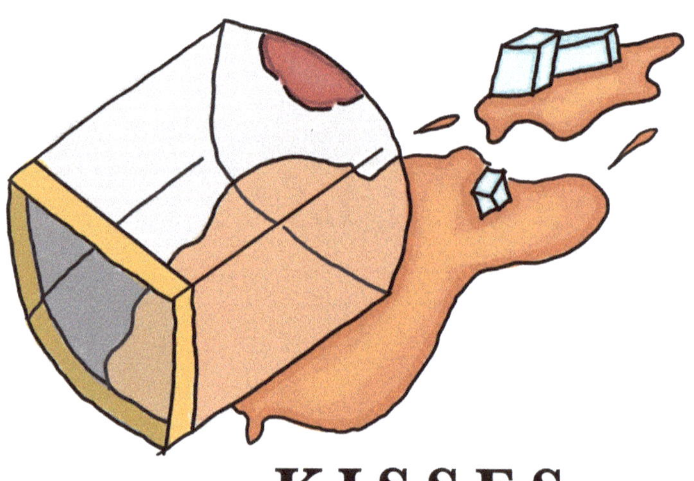

WHISKEY

KISSES

Here I am again, so into you.
Those lips, that smile,
those drunken kisses
that my sober mouth can taste.

The way your voice sounds
when you talk and laugh.
How you pick on me because we are different
and yet have a soft spot to let me in.

And your scent.
I love your scent.
The way you smell makes me high.

Oh, and when you kiss me,
I am breathless.
I let go.

Your heart could be my home.
I could really love you.
If only you would let me.

And if you love me,
let me know,
because I really don't have to go.

FINDING MYSELF AGAIN

I started to lose who I was when I found you.
I am starting to rediscover myself
despite being with you.

SPRING
TIME

The flowers are blooming,
maybe I will start blooming too.

QUERER

I can't wait to touch your skin.
Lose myself in the way you feel.
Dissolve into you as you hold me in.
I wonder what you smell of.

How your lips will feel when they kiss mine.
The taste of your skin on the tip of my tongue.
You on top of me, nails into your skin.
Our bodies, how they would intertwine.

Quiero sentirte
encima de mí.
Déjame amarte.
Emborracharme de ti.

MY PERSON

Where are you?
What do you look like?
I want to know your dreams and goals.
I want to know who you are
and what made you the way you are.

I am ready for love.
I am ready to find you.
I have so much to give you.
I will cook for you.
Take care of you when you are sick.

I want to grow with you and not apart.
Create memories that will last.
I dream of a family, a home
and the peace that comes from stability.

Please don't hurt me.
I want to know what it is like
for someone to truly love me.
I don't want to go through another heartbreak.
I barely survived the last one.

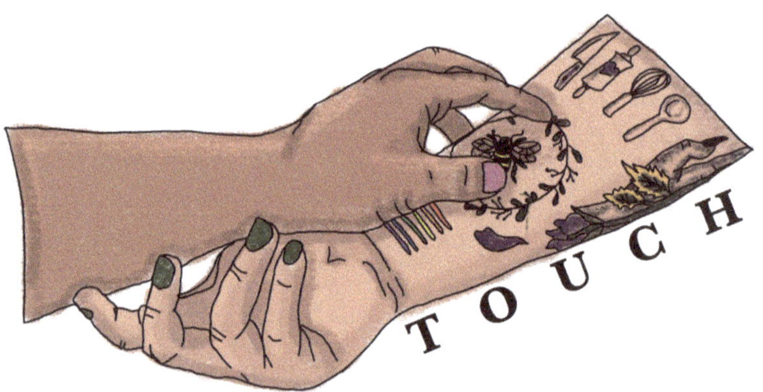
TOUCH

I didn't know I was starving until I met you.
The way your fingertips traced my thighs.
How your hands wandered throughout my body.
How your eyes were intimately staring into mine.

No one has ever touched me
or looked at me in the way that you do.

POTENTIAL

They say bad things
happen to good people
and here I am,
a good person.

I am not defined
by what has happened to me,
so, take me as I am,
as I am more than this.

I could be the one,
if you give me a chance.
You could be the good
that I deserve.

And I promise,
I have a heart filled
with so much love to give.
Searching for its forever home.

So,
please,
be my home.
I've been waiting my whole life for this.

COMING
TO
FRUITION

Imagine,
you are cleaning the dishes
and I wrap my arms around your waist
from behind you.

Picture this,
many stolen kisses.
A pleasant surprise,
just because.

Envision,
you are driving.
I, in the passenger seat,
massaging your back.

Dream of the day
where you and I
have grown together,
old and frail.

Sitting on our porch
with our morning coffee.
Looking back on our memories,
on the life we have built together,

in complete bliss.

I ADORE YOU

If only I could describe your laugh
and the way it warms my heart,
or how when I make you smile,
it is infectious in the best way.

The way your skin illuminates
at night
from the lights of your front porch.

And the joy I find
in listening to you,
watching you,
and seeing you.

If only you knew
that after each interaction
I am pining for more of you.
In hopes that you will stay
longer than just for the meantime.

LONG DISTANCE

I'm Still Healing - Koko Escoto

On the other side of the phone,
over 200 miles away,
how can I feel you
the way that I do?

I can only imagine
how your lips taste.
How your skin feels
when pressed up against mine.

But it's not just physical
because with only your voice
I can feel you
without you touching me.

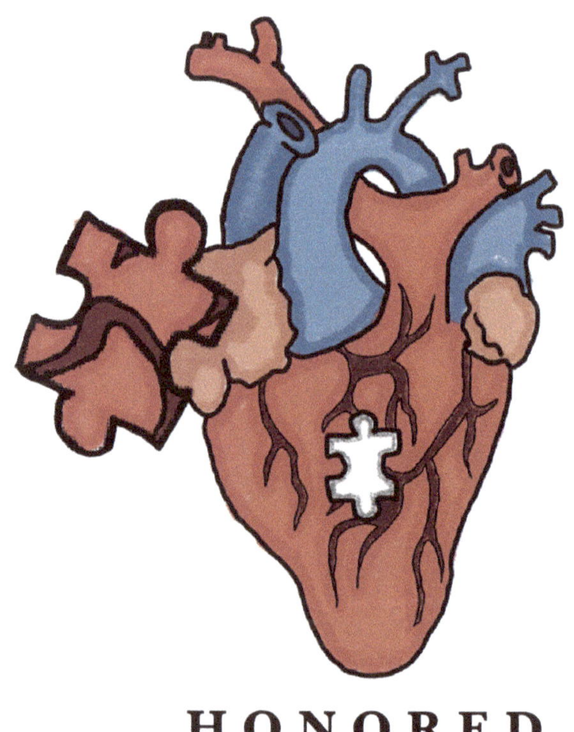

HONORED

In that moment
there was nothing more
I'd rather be
than to be yours.

What a privilege it is
to be a part of your world.

FRAGILE

She was reassuring,
open to learning,
non-judgmental.

She felt an utmost respect for me,
for my vulnerability,
and my trust in her.

If there ever was an example
of unconditional love
put into a moment,
this was it.

I am safe here.

MORE THAN

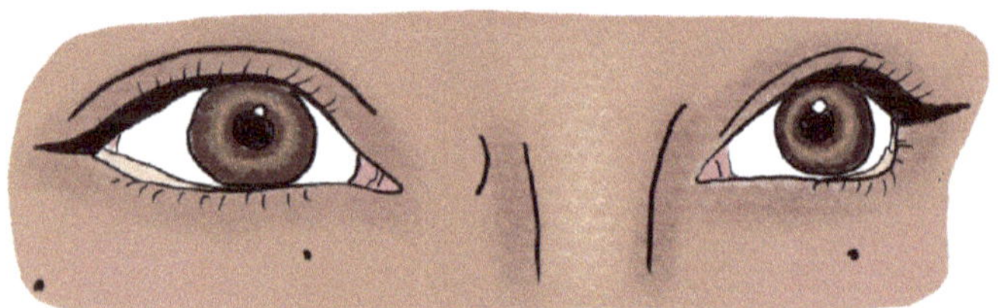

HER PARTS

Her eyes,
intimate and yearning,
vulnerability showing.

Her touch,
warm and loving,
sensations flowing.

Her voice,
calm and soothing,
security blooming.

The entirety of her being,
I surrender.

We are growing.

TO BE
LATINA

They adore my light caramel skin.
Eyes, brown honey in the light.
Dark, curly hair.

Asking to hear me speak,
sexualizing my Spanish.

Fascinated with my culture.
Eager to learn my language.
A constant reminder
that the idea of me is fetishized.

And this is what it's like
to date as a Latina.

HOPELESS
ROMANTIC

I am waiting for a love
filled with morning kisses,
soft touch in passing.
Intentional affection.

Cooking in the kitchen together,
occasional bickering
in a home that feels safe,
warm and fulfilling.

The security in sharing similar goals and dreams.
Excitement to start a family.
Helping each other grow,
and breaking our intergenerational traumas.

Most importantly,
committing the remainder of our lifetime
to cherish and love each other
in sickness and in health.

DELICATE

I must water her like a flower,
tend to her as I would a garden.

DESIRE

Feel me with intention
and touch me with assertion.
Grip my thighs
and put your hands around my throat.
Force me into submission.
Coerce me to be
yours.

THE HEARTACHE

Trigger warning

The following poetry depicts domestic violence (physical abuse, emotional abuse, and verbal abuse), PTSD and the healing process after it.

Proceed with caution and please engage in self-care while reading the upcoming poems.

National domestic violence hotline: 800-799-7233

MODIFICATION

Does it ever cross your mind
that I modify the way
I answer your questions
because I already know
what you don't want to hear.

I fear that if I tell you how I feel,
you're going to do
what you say you would.
You would just leave me.

I say "I don't know."
because I want you in my life
for as long as you let me have you.

So, how am I naïve?
I see long term,
not forever,
nor do I see you as temporary.

But I hope it's a long time
because I don't know what forever is,
I don't know what love is.

And fuck,
I like you so much,
it scares me to lose you.

COSTUMBRE

My Father,
he was abusive,
just like you.

I left a home of abuse
to build one with you.

HEAVY

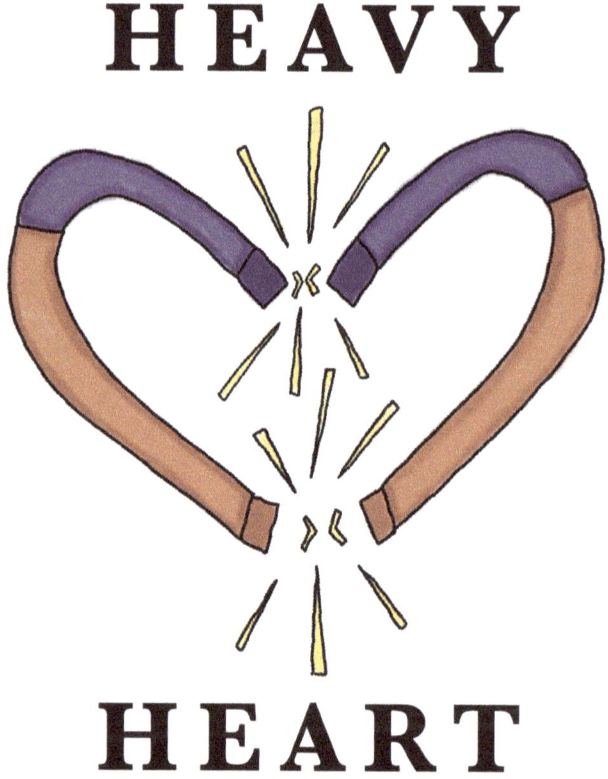

HEART

The guilt to dream of a life without you
is paralyzing when I know that I should leave.
Yet,
I can't help
that every **inch** of me
wants to stay.

OUT OF PLACE

There is a lack of belonging
in a home we once called ours.
Defined as a stranger
In my own home.

OUTGROW

We grew so far apart,
and there is nothing
I could ever do to repair
The disconnect between you and I.

WITHERING

Lately it has been hard
to give you every inch and effort in me.
I have nothing left.
I am dry and there is all this rain
seeping out from the cracks of my body.

Your words have broken me down
to the point that giving you all of me is harder to do.
It is almost a habit,
a habit of loving you unconditionally.

Lately I have been realizing that this relationship
is acid that burns my skin,
words that punch like fists,
and threats that manipulate my mind.

LET
ME
GO

I have to say this,
if you love me then why do you hurt me?
That is not love.
If you loved me,
you would end this.

You would end us like those words
that spout from your mouth
that throw jabs at me,
making me black and blue.

All that strength and breath
you waste on repeatedly cutting me down
to where I feel so little
when you can cut the strings
that our relationship is dangling from.

You have enough strength to hurt me.
You have enough strength to set me free.

So, here are the scissors.
Let me hit the ground.
You did this to us.

You wouldn't leave an animal
you've injured to slowly die.
You would rid it of its misery.

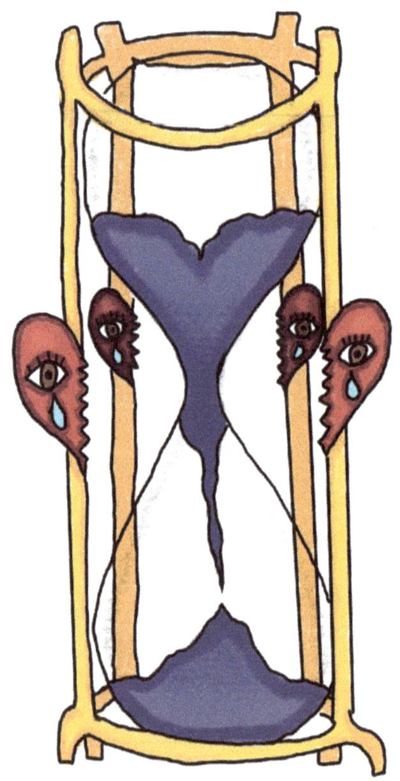

I
ALREADY
MISS
YOU

When I look at the life we have built together,
I realize that what we have
is more than we can handle.
I walk through our home
and it no longer feels like mine.
You have taken that privilege away from me.

I look at you and I love you immensely.
My body aches and I want to cry.
I wonder when you lost respect for me.
I wonder if you feel sorry,
if you feel anything at all
when you threaten me, call me names, insult me,
and see me cry.

I know that I am not perfect,
but I wish you could love me
the way that you say you do.

Now, we are more intimate
knowing that our relationship will
and must come to an end.
I will miss the touch of your skin.
Your kisses on my lips and body.

I wanted to grow old with you.
I don't know how to stop.
I am still in love with you,
but this is not love.
You do not hurt the ones you love.

When did you fall out of love with me?

COMING
TO AN
END

Am I afraid of being alone
or is my heart truly breaking?

I can't eat.
I can't breathe.
I can't sleep.
I can't think.

This is the end,
isn't it?

OUT
OF
LOVE

"I'm stuck with you."

And that's when it hit me,
you must not love me anymore.

TREAT ME
BETTER

Your words,
they hit me where it hurts.
Trigger memories.
Trigger emotions.
All of which are too familiar.

You are supposed to love me.
You are not supposed to hurt me.
I don't remember a time when you didn't treat me poorly.

When did you stop loving me?
Did you ever start?

STAY

It is true.
My life would change without you.
Yours would change without me too.
I didn't give you enough time to be alone.

You had so much growing to do.
We had so much growing to do.

Is this a sign that maybe we are not meant to be?
What do we keep fighting for?
What is there even left?
Is it for love?
Has there ever been love?

I know that we are far from healthy.
Yet, we stay together.
For what?

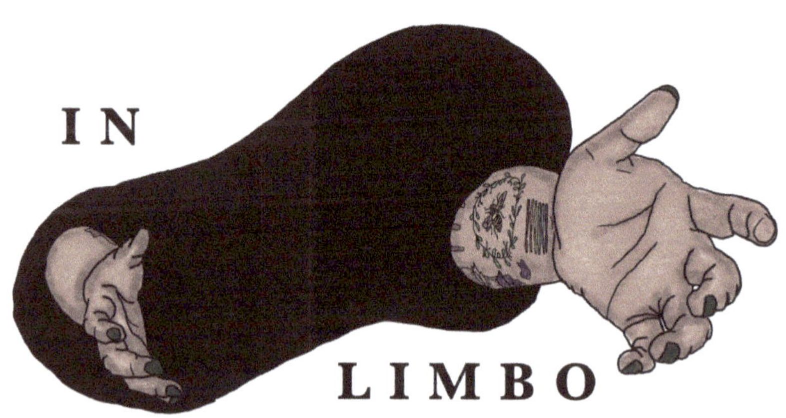
IN
LIMBO

It's almost like reaching in the dark
in search of comfort
and not being able to find it.

It's like you're underwater
starving to breathe
and deep inside
you know that if you do
you'll drown.

It's the feeling of wanting and not receiving.

The constant wonder,
is this... how love is supposed to feel?

THE
DAY
I
LEFT

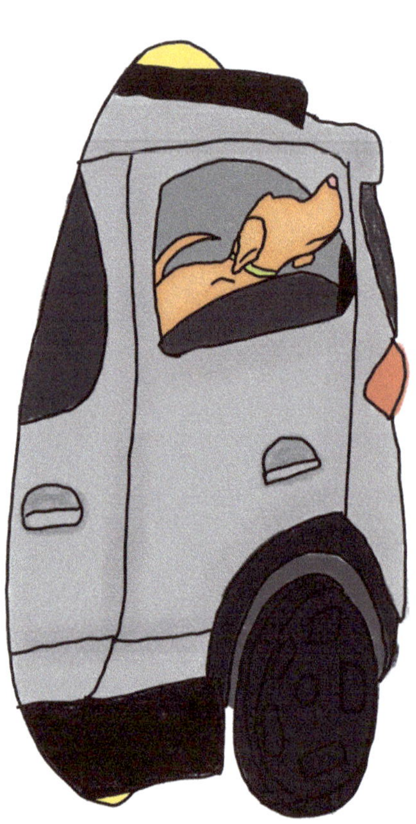

A Saturday,
at the end of May.
You called as I drove away.
Begging for me to stay.
For so many years,
My heart had reached for you.
With each time I waited for you to change,
but now it is too late.
In the end,
I did not crawl back to you
like I did
summer of 2014.

72 HOURS

A pair of pants, ripped from my hands,
thrown past me.
I was scared to ask how to fold them.
A recollection.
I was a *"selfish bitch"* who didn't know how to listen.
Laundry,
A constant reminder of the hell I lived in.

I didn't deserve to be called a piece of shit
or screamed at inches from my face.
"You stupid fucking bitch."
At 6 AM.

I didn't deserve
the collection of names
I held in your head.

Now look at us,
it is day 3
since I left.

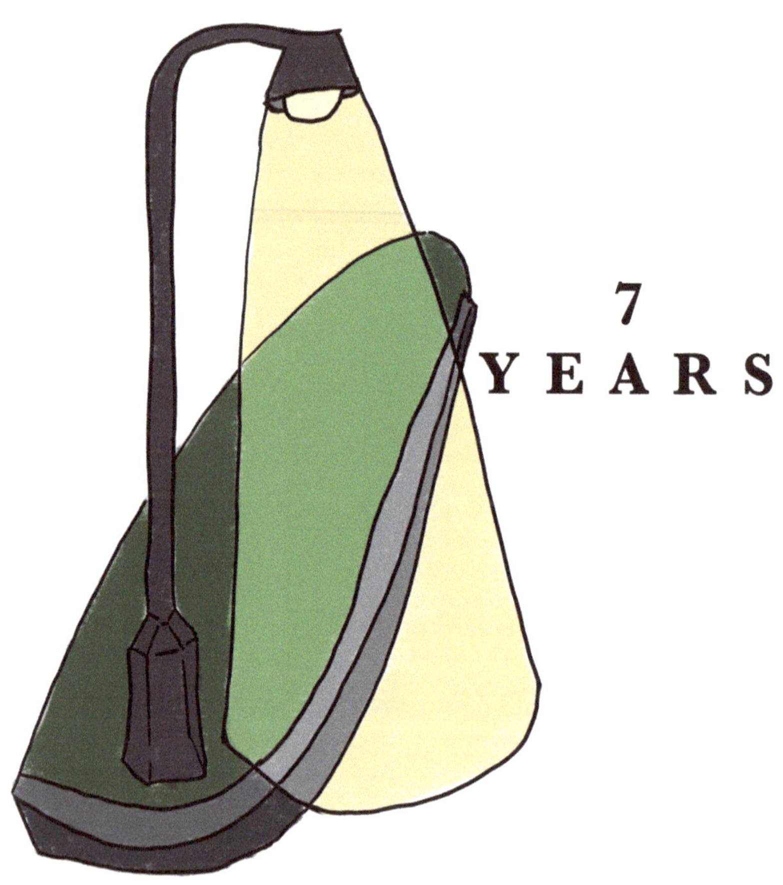
7
YEARS

How can you love someone
and treat them so poorly?
How can you expect them to stay?

17 DAYS
(Since I Left)

Who am I
without you?
My whole life was *you*.

All I ever wanted was **YOU.**

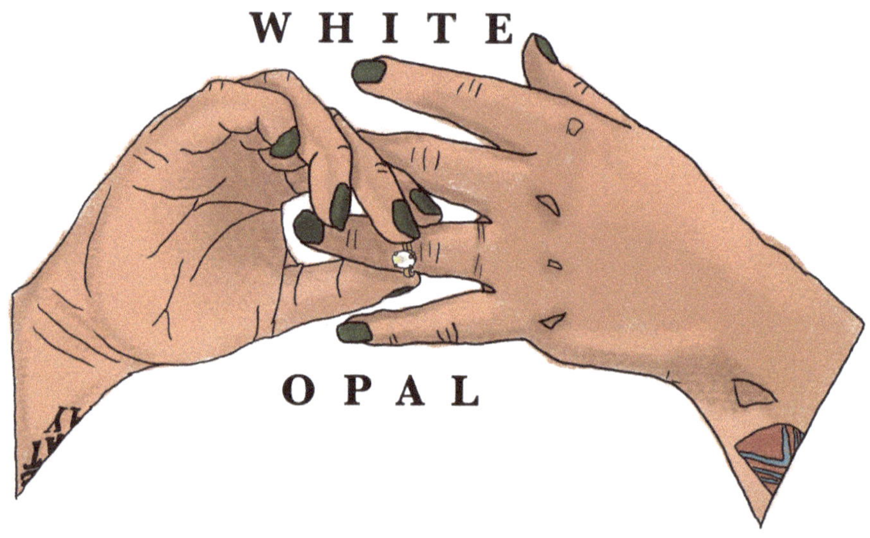
WHITE
OPAL

The symbolism of that ring
was not commitment,
but pain.

And now it is gone,
and I feel like I'm missing something.
As if I've lost something.

Tell me it gets easier.

A
I LOVED
YOU

It wasn't long until I realized
I wasn't hard to love,
you just didn't want to love me.

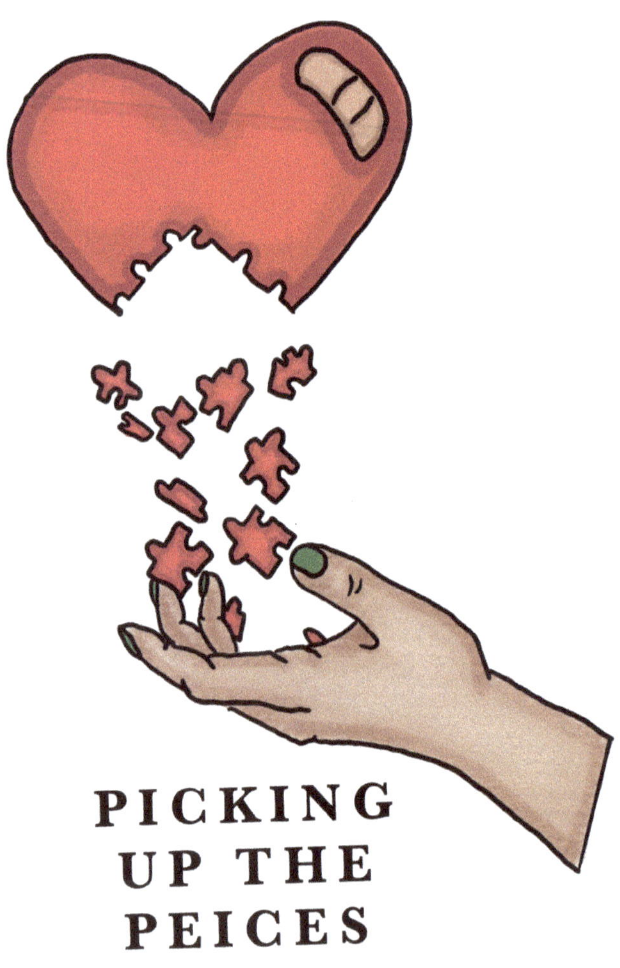

PICKING
UP THE
PEICES

Today, I learned that
you're in a relationship.

I am not sad about it,
but I am angry.

Angry that I am left to heal
from the damage that you have caused me.
I am left to go to counseling.
To fix all the damage you have done to me,
that I have to repair.
That I must grow from,
and it's affecting all my relationships.

Meanwhile, you are moving on.

I am not sad that you are in love.
My heart just aches
because I have to fix myself *again*.

FROGS

Our lips touch.
I feel detached.
Something's off.
You're not the one.

So many women,
countless kisses,
and yet not one
has been intoxicating.

Oh how I still believe
that when I find her,
a single kiss
will awaken the parts of me
yearning to love again.

IN ANOTHER LIFE

I could've had a good life with her.
Financial stability, a home, a comfortable life,
but it had to come with an emotional price.
I just couldn't do it anymore.

I had to show up for myself.
I had to love myself.

RECIPROCATION

I'm Still Healing - Koko Escoto

I am no longer giving my all
to people who don't give their all to me.
The energy they give to me
is the energy I give back to them.

I don't have time for people
that do not make time for me.

SELF-DEFENSE

"You ran away."

I gave her a look and said,
 "No, **YOU** ran me away."

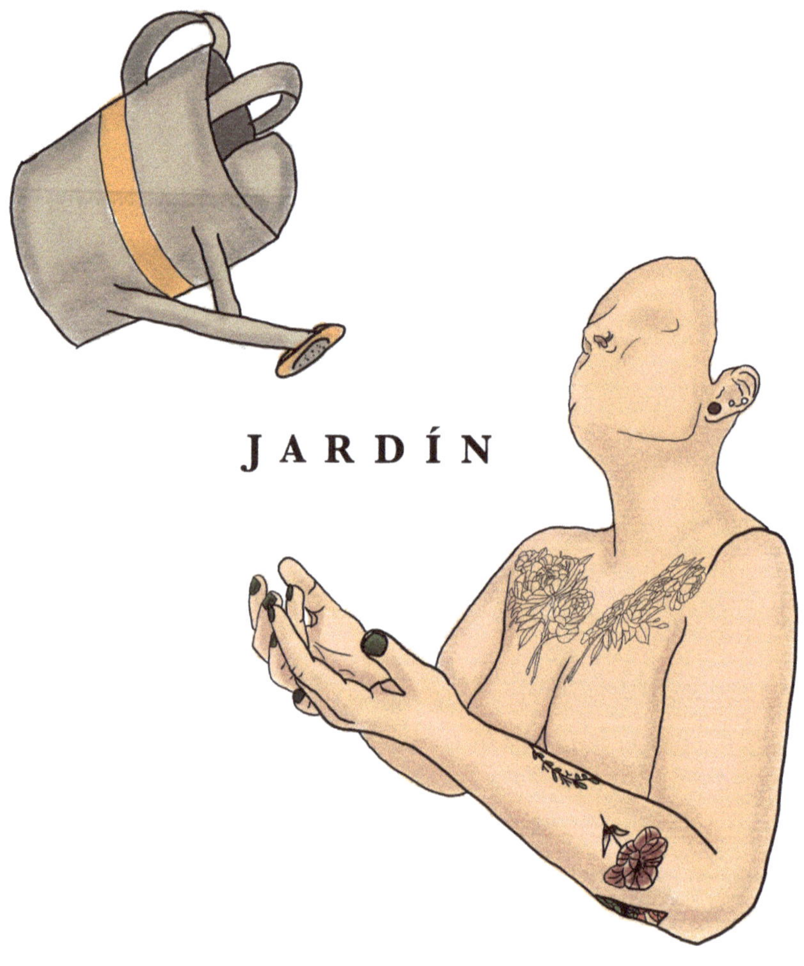

JARDÍN

I am a whole garden
and I'm not being watered.
My flowers are beginning to wilt
and my soil is starting to dry.

Love is my nutrition.
Consistency is my water.
Do not say you love me
when you cannot give me what I need.

Por favor,
soy un Jardín.
No se te olvide regarme.

MAY

When I left,
who would've thought
my world would have changed
the way that it did.

From home owning
to apartment living.
From living together
to living on my own for the first time.
One of the biggest challenges,
one of my greatest milestones.
The very thing you thought I was incapable of doing.

So, how does it feel to know
that I can live without you?

And now it's been a year.
I thought I'd never stop loving you.
I thought I'd regret leaving you.
It was the best decision I have ever made.

Because leaving you
was self-defense.
Leaving you
was an act of self-love.

PHOTOGRAPHS

I'm Still Healing - Koko Escoto

Memories of us,
like a ghost in the corner of my mind.
In the deepest crevices
of my heart.

I remember the laughter.
I remember the smiling.
Oh how 7 years felt like a lifetime with you,
but it is all so foreign to me now.

And I'm beginning to forget
how hard I fought for us.
The tears and the agony it was to love you.
What a shame it was for us to part.

Memories,
whether written or photographed,
I don't recognize us anymore.
Pictures of us break my heart.

In the end,
you gave me no choice.
I had to kill us.

Because while you were breaking my heart,
I had to break it with you.

ABYSS

Mind is racing.
Thoughts are scattered.
In this skin,
I feel trapped.

Take me out
of this body.

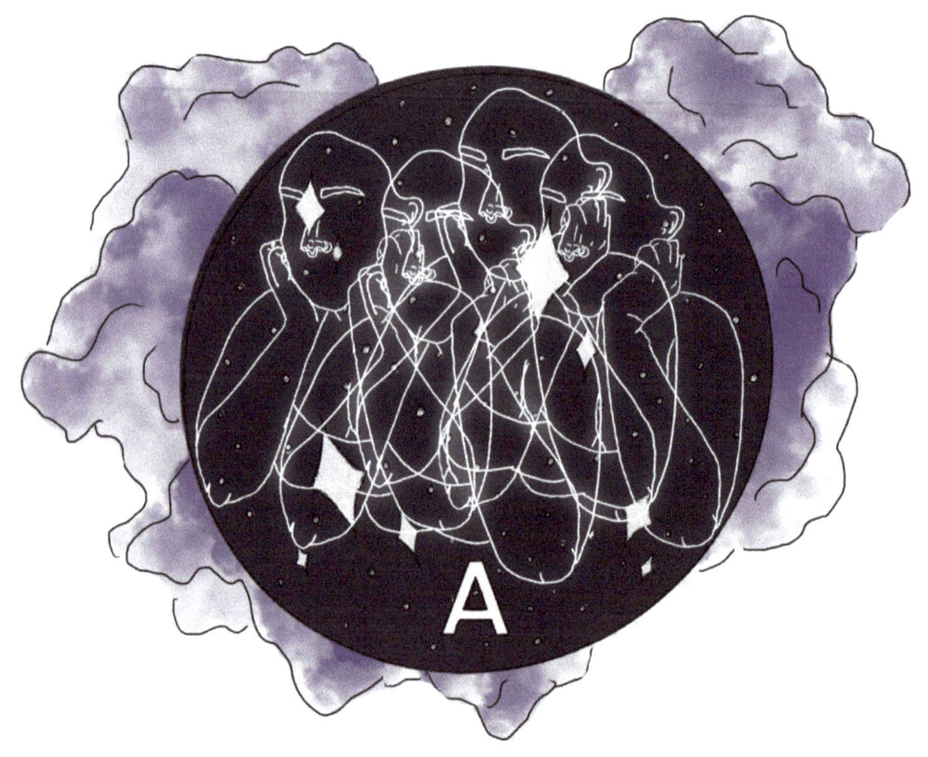
A

I might still love her.
I think I will always love her.
Maybe I just love the idea of her…
That made up person in my *fucking* head
that truly loved me.

3 9 2 6

A final steppingstone
where I can feel my heart swelling,
and preparing to break.
Again.

And I remind myself
that I may have loved her,
but this house
it was not a home.

I remember the yelling,
all the name calling,
the threatening,
and the barricading of the front door.

Yet, even through it all,
I still loved her
but just like me
the house must go.

And so here it is,
the last string
holding us together.

Our final goodbye.

CHANGES

It's like the world keeps moving
but I am not ready.
I am scared to enter this new life,
a life I never thought I'd be in.

A nightmare.
Please wake me up.
I don't want to say goodbye
to the girl that I once was.

And I can see her
but her memory is distant.
I don't recognize her anymore.
She is no longer me.

I am not ready
but it's time to rediscover who I am,
to relearn to love myself
and to grow into this new world.

GHOST
2014-2021
L
2008-2022

I can't bear the thought
that I still love you.
That you cross my mind from time to time,
but yet it's not you that I love.

It's who you could have been,
who I deserved you to be.
Not who you were,
and not who you are.

REMNANTS OF YOU

I've been waiting patiently for you to fade.
For you to no longer plague my thoughts,
but the memory of you still lingers.
An aftertaste on my tongue.

And someone or something
will awaken your memory,
set fire to the pieces of you,
that you left behind.

Again, I will wait for you to disintegrate
into the deepest darkest corners of my mind.
Where I can hear my heart breaking
because in those moments it yearns for us.

And it begs for understanding.
For the truth of who I was to you
because how could you have loved me,
and hurt me at the same time?

And I wish you knew
that if you had changed,
I would have loved you forever.

HAPPY
BIRTHDAY,
10
DAD

I've watched you age
through photographs and videos.
You have gray hair now.
Where has the time gone?

And yet, you have not grown.
You tell everyone you miss me.
My name even slips from your mouth.
My heart aches in your absence.

I will never forget
when you said
"I don't need you."
And "leave, you are not welcomed here."

You ripped my heart out of my chest
when I begged for you to be in my life,
and you set that letter on fire
in front of me.

And mom says to forgive you,
that you don't have much time left,
that you are my father,
but what about me?

I am your daughter.

4 5 8
D A Y S

(Since I left)

I'm Still Healing - Koko Escoto

As I continue to heal from the trauma of our love,
I have come to the realization
of why it's so hard for me to move on
and it's because when I left
I wasn't finished loving you.

And my body,
it continues to hold onto the remnants of you
and it pains me to see
that I do not affect you in that way.

So,
after all this time,
I think we now know
who loved who most.

GROWTH

I equate love with contempt and chaos
for it is the only love I know,
and now I must mend these wounds.
The ones you never let heal.

I will continue to write about you,
until I finally let you go.
I will no longer be in contact with you,
and maybe, finally, I can move on.

So,
starting today,
I must accept the fact
that you never truly loved me.

Because as I grow,
I'm beginning to understand
that love is not disrespectful nor damaging.

INNER CHILD

There is a heaviness within my chest as I mourn.
This heart has gradually grown barren,
and my eyelids feel dense and lethargic.
The entirety of my body
craves a substance it has never had.

My inner child is starving for love.

HOMESICK

I was in our hometown.
The streets were unfamiliar
and still, all I could see
was the ghost of you.

Ashamed to yearn someone
who caused my heart great suffering.

And despite this,
I felt homesick
for the person I begged you to be.

I am still healing.

STAGE FIVE: ACCEPTANCE

I dreamt that you died last night
and I heard that means
it is completely over.

So why am I still grieving?

Some days I feel like I am thriving.
Other days I feel like I am stuck.

And before I know it,
it will be two years since I left,
and I know that the love I had for you was real.
Was it real for you too?

But I must come to terms with this.
My questions will remain unanswered.
My closure will never be satisfied.

I just wish you could admit to fault,
for the damage you caused.
To just hear my story
but there is no benefit in spilling my heart out to you.

I must accept the fact that I left
even though I still loved you.

PHANTOM AFFECTION

Never have I heard a silence
to be so loud.
Never have I felt a distance
to cut so deep.

I would have given you
every little bit of me.
Up to every last drop.
All of me.

What a fool I was
to think that you wanted me.

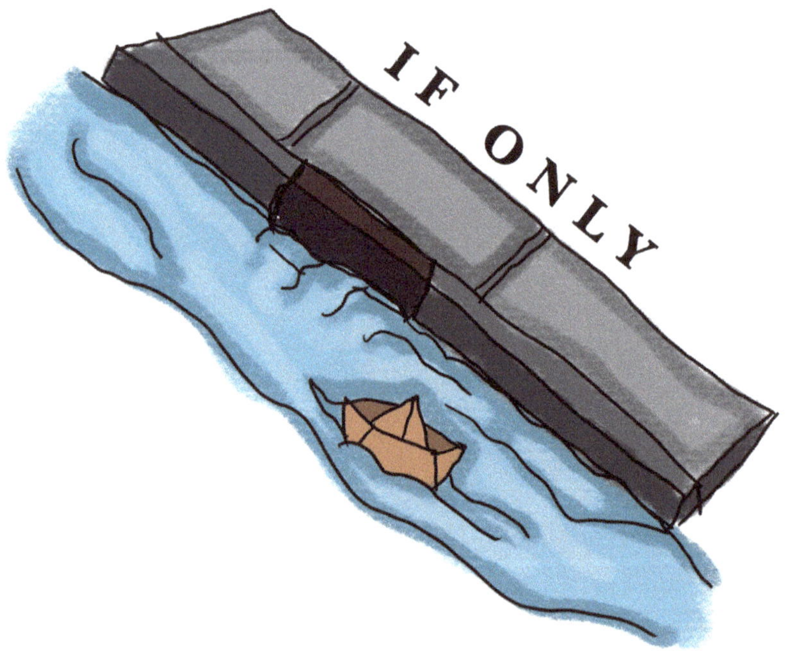
IF ONLY

To not know what I want
is an oxymoron
when all I've ever dreamt of
is to be loved.

CONSTANT CRAVING

I wonder how you are sometimes.
I wonder if you ever think of me too.
Do I cross your mind?
Do I make your heart ache?
And just when I think I am over you,
I stumble a few steps backward.
Wishing we could have somehow gone right.

But no,
we went so wrong,
and it wasn't a fast demise
because I gripped onto you
for dear life.

The time proceeded to pass
and every year I tried to grasp onto you
but you were never truly there.
You saw me as someone who was vulnerable
and you took advantage
of the profound love I had for you.

I would have done anything for you.
I was just a little girl,
wishing to gain your approval,
to earn your love.

So, I sustained all the jabs and the screaming.
I embraced you every time you said you hated me,
called me a bitch, a cunt, a piece of shit.
Even when you slapped my chest, threw shoes at me,
shoved me,
and told me I deserved it.

I loved you through it all.

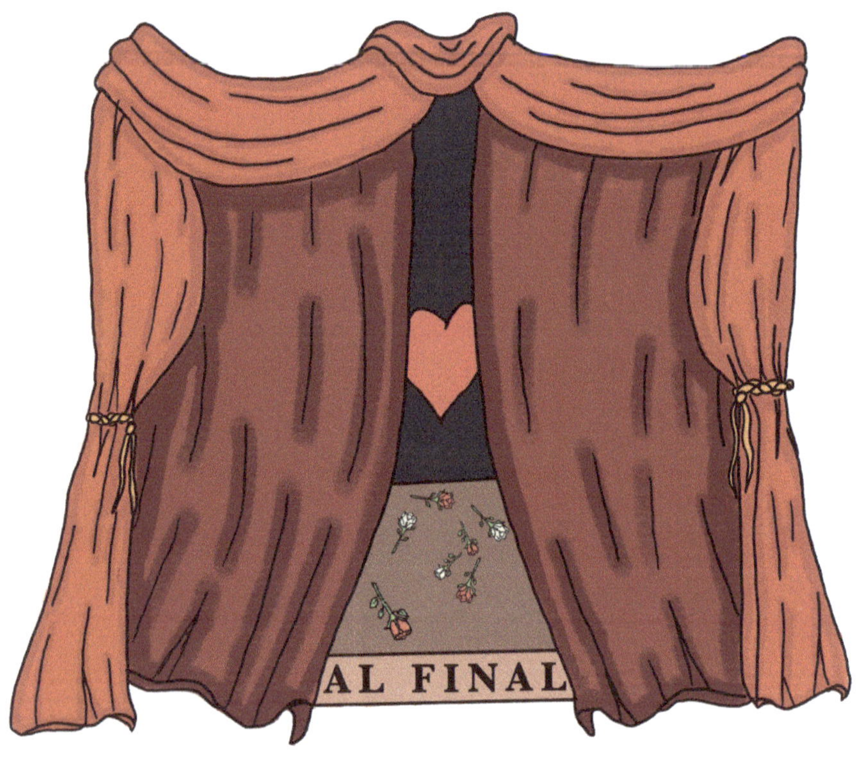
AL FINAL

You were the kind of love
that made me think I didn't know how.

One I craved and fought so hard to obtain.

Pero últimamente,
fuiste un tipo de amor que no era.

MISSED

CALL

I was deleting old voicemail
when I stumbled upon two from you,
both were a couple days after I left.
I knew I shouldn't have listened to them.

Over a year has passed since those messages,
and the wound in my chest has yet to fully heal.
Hearing you tremble in tears,
crying for me to come back.

Pleas that opened the locked door
of feelings I had buried away.
The pain that had consumed my body.
Now these wounds are covered in salt.

YOU
ARE
FADING

I have forgotten bits and pieces of you.

The sound of your voice,
the taste of your lips.
The smell of your skin,
and the feel of your touch.

I have forgotten
how I loved you
or if you ever loved me.

But I didn't forget
how you made me feel
unlovable,
unworthy,
and miniscule.

Now,
only triggers
remind me of you.

D R U N K E N

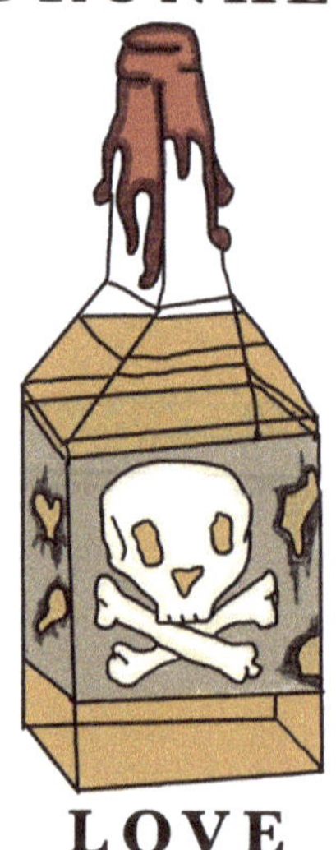

L O V E

Walking into that pizzeria
In love the moment I laid eyes on her.
I can't recall the words that were said.
But I remember the red hair and her scent.

It wasn't long before she disappeared.
To say, *"come over."* months later, at 3 am.
Like the fool that I was, 20 and dumb,
I surrendered to her call.

Little did I know,
This was the start of our story.

I remember her,
inebriated, in the fetal position on her bed.
It's Always Sunny in Philadelphia
playing in the background,
the whiskey seeping through her skin.

It wasn't until later, I learned
That she wouldn't remember me in the morning.
Alcohol, a common theme,
consumed her.

3 am, I snuck over.
She wasn't there.
Panicked, no answers.
She called the following morning.
Her second DUI.
"Will you be my girlfriend?"
20, dumb and in love,
I said, *"yes."*

Despite it being her rock bottom,
She knew I would do anything for her.
A testament,
of the one-sided, unconditional love, I held for her
that she was never sober enough to reject.

Fast forward 9 years,
It has been two years since I left.
And I'm burdened with memories
That are of no use to me anymore.
Yet, I can't help but think:
What about me
was not worth changing for?

SLEEP TALKING

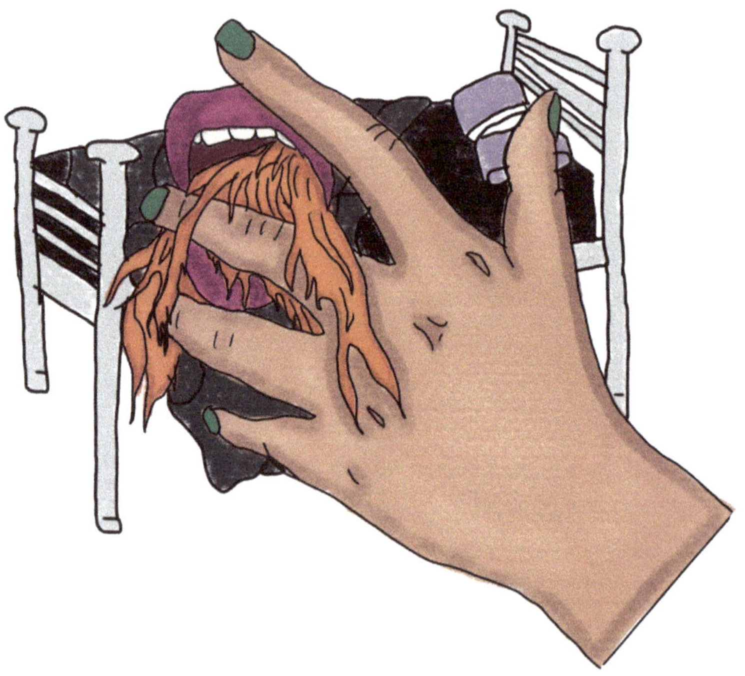

In the middle of the night,
I was sound asleep
when I turned over and held her tight,
right after I called out your name.

I don't recall dreaming of you,
or dreaming at all.
I wouldn't have known
if she wasn't lying in my bed.

Oh how daunting it is to think
you had cut so deeply
that you run actively
in the subconscious of my mind.

REFLECTION

I've been looking deep into myself,
rummaging through the trauma
that I've stored in the attic of my mind.
Several boxes, unpacking and reliving.

I am trying to understand why
I see red flags
and I run towards them.

Is it a lack of self-love?

Or maybe it's because I still don't know what love is
and I catch myself wanting to fall back into old habits.
To change myself, because maybe, just maybe,
then someone will love me.

And the more I reflect on who I am,
and who I've been,
I can feel that little girl
in my head
begging on her knees,

"Can someone please love me?"

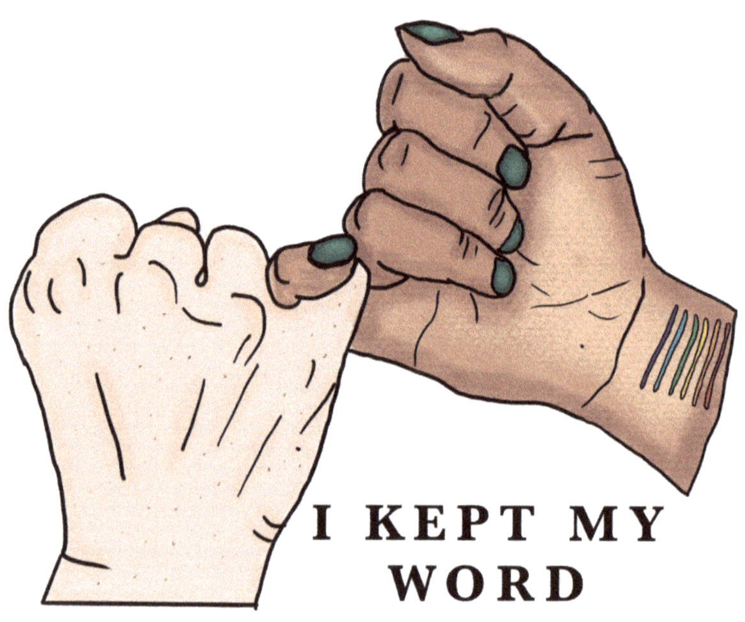
I KEPT MY
WORD

I remember when you said,
"Please don't ever leave me."
I held you close, and I promised
that the only way I would leave you
was only if you left me.

Fast forward 7 years and it's a memory of you
filling me up with loving words,
proclaiming that I am the love of your life.
That this time you will try to change.

But in the end
I had to protect myself.
I built a wall that not even I could take down,
hoping it would hurt less when I left.

And for almost 2 years,
the guilt I had carried
to leave a person I promised to love forever
consumed me.

Until I finally realized
that each time you called me names,
screamed in my face, watched me cry,
and said I deserved it,

You had already left me.

JADED

If this break up has taught me anything,
it is that I will never truly love as greatly
or as freely.
Again.

The next person
will not be an unapologetic love.
But it will be a love
that was good enough.

And whoever you are,
I'm sorry in advance.
Please forgive me,
I promise to love you
the best I can.

THERAPY

Today,
for the first time in years,
you were not the main subject
in therapy.

A milestone
I didn't realize I needed to reach.

Oh, how heartwarming
it is to know
that you can no longer hurt me
anymore.

LEFT BEHIND

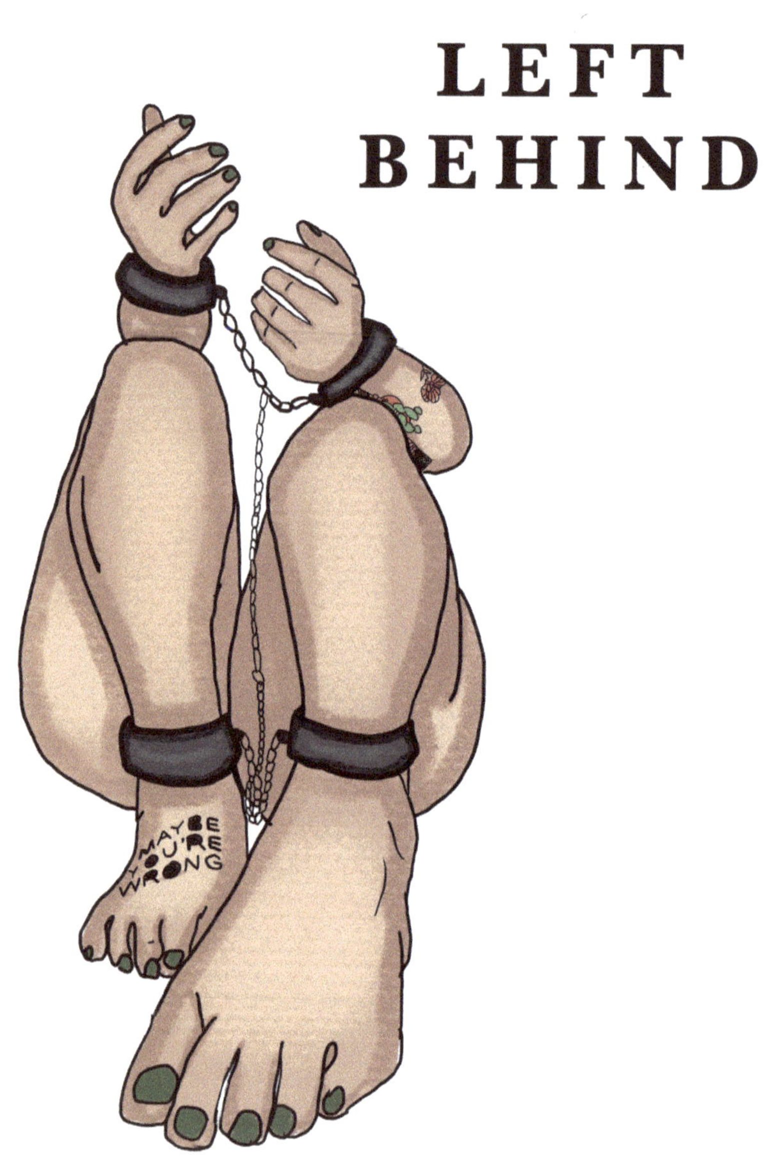

I think I figured out why
I don't like to be alone.
She has become an infestation
Of memories I want to erase.

I still remember her favorite color,
the whiskey on her breath.
I still remember the way she danced,
the mannerisms I want to forget.

And It's not that I still love her
But in the silence
I can still hear her.
And It's not that I still miss her
but in an empty room,
I can still feel her.

In two years,
you'd think the pain from loving her
would fade away like most of my memories do.
And it's not that I'm not over her
or maybe it is just that.

And I sit in this dark room, alone,
and I wonder,
why can't I leave her
when I've already left her?

The flashbacks live inside me.
They come in waves.
And the images, they are blurry.
Out of place.
I can't formulate the words
but I can still hear you.

Core memories.
You are gripping my wrists
toward your chest
to call me names.
The loud punch of the dashboard.
When you threw shoes at me.
The disbelief when you slapped my chest.
The sound of your scream.

The breath I lost
when your words punched like fists.

"Shut the fuck up."
"Stupid fucking bitch."
"Piece of shit."
"I hate you."

And under the same breath,
"You're the love of my life."
You knew just how to hurt me.

The disrespect
when all I did was
fight to love you.
All the while
you simply smiled
as I turned black and blue.

ACCEPTING THE

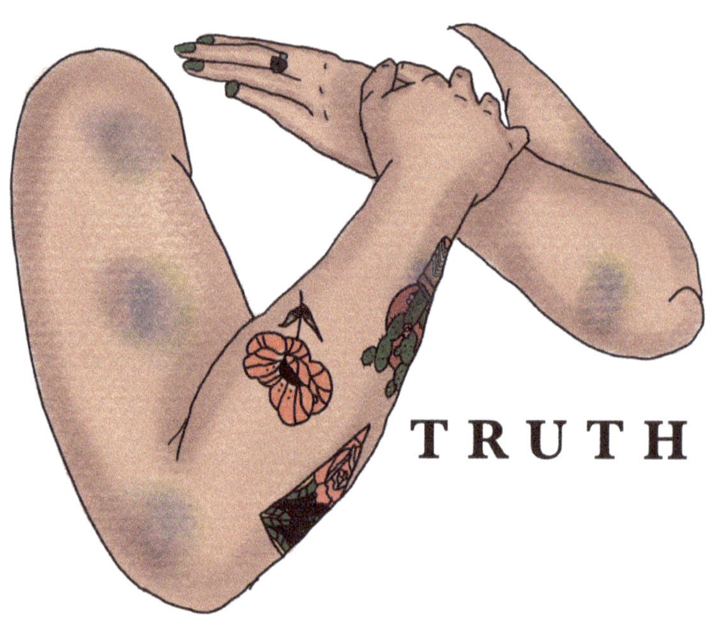

TRUTH

In 3 months,
it'll be two years since I left
and I used to say:
"We broke up."
Minimizing the strength I had to leave.

Early on,
someone would ask why I left
and I would say:
"She's a good person.
She just wasn't nice to me."
Desensitizing my experience.

I now sit with this heaviness in my chest,
because in order for me to break the cycle,
I must call it what it was:
Domestic abuse.

From now on,
I am taking back the narrative.
It is a privilege to love me

One by one,
each photograph
held a memory
I could never erase.
Each photograph
had emotions
that only I could taste.

I'm Still Healing - Koko Escoto

The kitchen,
where I baked
Cookies, donuts
and her favorite,
Sticky buns.
I can still smell
the sweetness
engulfing the summer air,
and the freedom I felt
in loving her.

The hallway
to the bedroom,
laundry basket thrown
to the floor.
I can still hear her
in the bedroom,
name calling,
her favorite,
"Selfish bitch."
from across the hall.
A lingering pulling
of my heart
when I couldn't breathe.

Not only the memory of her,
but the haunting of our love
in the lime green
painted summer daffodil yellow
house.